# The Cup in Hand

# The Cup in Hand

A Balancing Act of Poems

Zai Xiaz

RESOURCE *Publications* · Eugene, Oregon

THE CUP IN HAND
A Balancing Act of Poems

Copyright © 2022 Zachary Sylvester. All rights reserved. Except for brief quotations in critical publications or reviews, no part of this book may be reproduced in any manner without prior written permission from the publisher. Write: Permissions, Wipf and Stock Publishers, 199 W. 8th Ave., Suite 3, Eugene, OR 97401.

Resource Publications
An Imprint of Wipf and Stock Publishers
199 W. 8th Ave., Suite 3
Eugene, OR 97401

www.wipfandstock.com

PAPERBACK ISBN: 978-1-6667-5442-1
HARDCOVER ISBN: 978-1-6667-5443-8
EBOOK ISBN: 978-1-6667-5444-5

10/21/22

To Hollie, Sam, Tate, and Landon

Special thanks to the copyeditor: Victoria Lane

# Contents

*Introduction* | ix

## Part One: Eyes Opened
    Thought I | 5
    *Apparent* | 6
    Thought II | 8
    *Molecruel* | 9
    Thought III | 12
    *WaveZ* | 13

## Part Two: The First Drop
    Thought IV | 17
    *Vociferous* | 18
    Thought V | 19
    *Mindsome* | 20
    Thought VI | 21
    *-the deadliest contagion-* | 22

## Part Three: Hate's Domination
    Thought VII | 25
    *The Wise Guise* | 26
    Thought VIII | 27
    *The Evil Genie* | 28
    *The Drowning Pool* | 30

## Part Four: Middle Ground
    Thought IX | 35
    *Blinded Fate* | 36
    Thought X | 38
    *Breeching* | 39
    *LoHatVe (Lo-Hat-Vay)* | 40

## Part Five: Singularity
    Thought XI | 45
    *Dream Girl* | 46
    *Our Freedom Cage* | 47
    *Forged* | 50

## Part Six: The Getting Up
    Thought XII | 53
    *The Eternal Epiphany* | 54
    Thought XIII | 55
    *The Bigot Tree* | 56
    Thought XIV | 59
    *Above* | 60

## Part Seven: As the Sun Sets
    Thought XV | 65
    *Dam of Reality* | 66
    *Fantastic Fabric* | 68
    Thought XVI | 69
    *Nine Out of Twelve* | 70

*Afterword* | 71
*Appendix: Mania Collection* | 73

# Introduction

What is love? That question sometimes takes a lifetime for one to answer fully. So far in my life, I have been able to summarize it as a culmination of positive emotions wrapped into one heart-striking (non-cerebral) feeling. One way to define it is that it is the opposite of hate. Hate is an ill will negatively impacting our thoughts and actions. Conversely, love can be described as a healthy will positively impacting our thoughts and actions. Simple? Not exactly. These two foundations for emotions, love and hate, are intrinsically complicated because they are the poles of complex human emotions. Love and hate need to be broken down and observed from various perspectives.

There are nine distinct types of love according to the ancient Greeks:

1. *Philia*: platonically affectionate love or deep-friendship love
2. *Pragma*: enduring love
3. *Eros*: romantic love
4. *Ludus*: playful love
5. *Storge*: familiar love or parent-child-dynamic love
6. *Philautia*: self-love
7. *Agape*: selfless love
8. *Mania*: obsessive love
9. *Xenia*: guest love or hospitality

Philia is the baseline of the nine loves. It is the love that develops with a sibling, a similar-aged relative, i.e., a cousin, or through early relationships such as friends at school.

Pragma is present with long-lasting love, such as a marriage or life-long best friend. It is a deeply embedded love that grows with ourselves and the relationship.

Eros is a physical love harvested as a sexual affection as opposed to philia's mental affection. It is fueled by hedonistic urges.

Ludus is the "I'm-falling-for-them" love. It is shown through flirtation and is the usual precursor to eros and intimate relations. Ludus is what animates the butterflies in our stomachs.

Storge is the love that we all hopefully encounter at birth. It is the innate, biological love between a parent and child. Although rooted in parental instinct, it is not monopolized by the parent-child relationship. A deep friendship or a master-apprentice relationship can possess storge.

Philautia is the love given to us by ourselves. It is the love that cycles through the id, ego, and superego. If the checks and balances of those three align, we crank the valve open to the love we provide for ourselves. It is also the healthy binding of the mind-body-soul dynamic.

Agape is the complete love of others and is difficult to achieve. Those lucky people born with a pure heart practice agape with ease. Others have to work to overcome demanding egos or trust issues due to fear and anxiety. Once one can love all unconditionally, one can master agape.

Mania is a destructive form of love; it is love to its extreme—anything to the extreme treads the line of unhealthiness. One must be wary of this love. It breaks the possessor down and falsely builds up the person being obsessed over. Usually a one-way street, this form of love ends in wreckage. Mania can also develop from extreme philautia in the form of narcissism.

Xenia is the love shown to a guest coming over to our home or new people in our lives. It is a courtesy love based on respect for others, even if they are strangers.

Love will generally be considered throughout the book as the positive influence of emotions. Some of the positive emotions are joy, hope, satisfaction, tranquility, and desire. Love creates the overall sense of synchronization with reality. This allows one to accept life. With this acceptance, one becomes free; this freedom begets happiness; happiness attracts others.

Hate can be broken into two distinct types: internal and external. Internal hate is self-loathing. External hate is the fear and anger we have for others. Our internal hate keeps the self-esteem buried with no flowers in the soil. Our external hate comes in different forms, such as prejudicial or familiar hate, i.e., hatred of an ex-partner.

Hate emboldens negative emotions. These include anger, sadness, fear, jealousy, and disgust. Hate warps reality to the point of delusion; it is the great deceiver. When hate dominates our emotions, it causes us to repulse others through anger, fear, and jealousy.

The catalysts of love and hate are good and evil, respectively. Through good, we promote love. Conversely, through evil, we promote hate. There is subjectivity in defining what is good and what is evil. But in certain cases, actions and ideas are objective: death of innocents is evil and driven by hate; helping others in need is good and driven by love.

There are a couple of paradoxical questions regarding love and hate. Can love be bad? Can hate be good? Love can be as destructive as hate if we allow it to forge too heavily. This weighty and destructive love, as described above as mania, can do the same damage to people as hate does. It is like an anchor of a ship caught on the seafloor. Once an apparatus of security, the anchor now holds the ship back from its progress. Hate can be good only if it describes the feeling against evil. But we must not use hate to combat evil. We must wield love against it to truly defeat it. Fighting fire with fire only produces larger flames. We must quench it with its polar opposite, water—that which is love.

Love can be taxing to discover if rarely exposed to it, or rediscover if lost. It is sometimes hidden from our view, like it is playing a round of hide-and-seek. It also requires patience and effort to possess and keep love. It is like love doesn't need us but enigmatically requires possession to exist. Hate needs a person to possess it.

It seeks us out like a deranged dog. Once it locks its jaws, we must fight to pry it away.

When it comes to polar emotions, we resemble black holes. Hate will rush into us. It will drop dead and heavy on us if we aren't vigilant and learned. It will swirl and sink deep. Hate knows this and takes advantage of it. We have to put effort into ridding ourselves of it through knowledge, experience, and betterment. Love, on the other hand, will dance along our horizons, kicking the quantum flux. We have to pull the love inside us. Once secured, it supernovas without an easy escape.

Love is the paramount connection. It is the fundamental bond of living creatures. Through our love for each other, we perpetuate life. Meanwhile, hate is in the business of destroying. It either wants us to lie down in a brittle and bitter state and wait for death or to destroy others. We can connect through hate, however, but it collects to ultimately destroy people. Love is the honest human gravitation; the strong human force attracting us together.

The idea of a cup in hand symbolizes the sometimes ridiculous balancing act (holding a cup by the base instead of gripping it evenly around the sides) between the positive and negative emotions of love and hate. This balance is binary in nature. If there was no hate, love could not be appreciated, and there would just be a neutral state of emotion. This entire book is composed of the balancing act within our lives. We cannot rid ourselves completely of negative emotions that coincide with hate and be full of total love, but we can balance them and make sure we do not become full of hate.

Both love and hate are easier to feel than they are to define. They are concepts that define themselves empirically and through compounding heuristics. We can sense them without difficulty, but defining them requires philosophic and creative measures. A pedantic definition cannot do either of them true justice. The following series of thoughts and poems intend to describe the various angles of love and hate to gain a tighter grasp on what they truly are through the feelings associated with them.

The Cup in Hand

# Part One
## Eyes Opened

# Thought I

At birth, love is supposed to flow through us like our first breath of air. We do not check for love; it is just expected. Is it a natural part of humanity? Or is it just something we imagine to cope with living with each other? Is hate the same abstraction only in our minds? Or are they natural forces?

Love is the backbone of positive emotions. As we come from innocent beginnings, we do not yet know what hate is unless we are born into extreme negligence and evil. Hate is something learned; love is provided to us by our parents and instinct. We have glimpses of hate through our spurts of developmental selfishness in our toddler years. But parental love, storge, has the power to absorb those negative emotions.

The following poem, *Apparent*, concerns storge love. This love is the assumed unconditional love. It is deeply interwoven into our survival instincts; we must care for and love our offspring. The love between parent and child is born with the child. This love is like a key to a door in the mind, unlocking a new instinct—a fresh, pure feeling.

# Apparent

To love without condition
The purity of it all
The joy of what we made
The culmination of what is us

Could be all of our worst qualities
Or all our finest
The love escapes us as the rays of light
    From the stars

You're now our everything
Where this love was housed
We cannot say
It is born like a twin—Siamese

To develop and destroy each other's diffidence
To build from babbles and nurture in nature
To learn together—for parents develop along
    The child

A child never separated from
Even after the umbilical's cleave
One's child must be connected to one's knees
Because their death takes them

The most natural yuanfen
Parent and child
Isn't it intuition?
Isn't it apparent?

The quickest and most unyielding
The bond rivaling covalent's
The love only known
By a family grown

# Thought II

Love can be extremely fickle; it comes and goes as it pleases. When it chooses to leave, hate seeks to fill the emptiness left behind. It "loves" to replace the void left by lost or forgotten love.

Acquiring hate is a sinecure. It is right around the corner, waiting to be incorporated to perpetuate despair, or at the very least, agitation. Hate is like the world's lowest hanging fruit, with the proverbial serpent snaking its way to deceive. Love is at the crown of the tree—the ultimate prize.

The following poem, *Molecruel*, deals with the fear of the unknown and impending isolation. It is a transition of positive emotions (love-based) to negative emotions (hate-based) back to positive.

The dominant love in the poem is philia. The bond of molecules is like a bond of siblings or close friends. The thought of losing that bond can conjure sadness, which can lead to despair. Hate enjoys feeding on despair, but the molecule must have hope. The act of breaking bonds and severing the philia relationship hurts, but there is light on the other side of the darkness. May it have the patience.

# Molecruel

This was it
My weight could no longer bear
Long fall from where I sit . . .
Viscous pain all around me
Vicious friction

Pulling on my existence
Or pushing on my determination
Hard to tell
I am giving up my place
My fall from grace

I'm being torn from my comrades
Alone with no control
Nothing to clutch
Just empty space
A dot on a page

As I waver and fall
I lose hope more and more
Am I part of the poor
Or a piece of richness?
I'm truly torn

The crash was abrupt
I rolled through darkness
But never broke
I wanted to accept my fate
Ignorant to its definition

As I slipped into a darker place
I felt a force pulling me up
I saw my comrades
We were together at last
Feeding into life

    The plant rich from the pour . . .

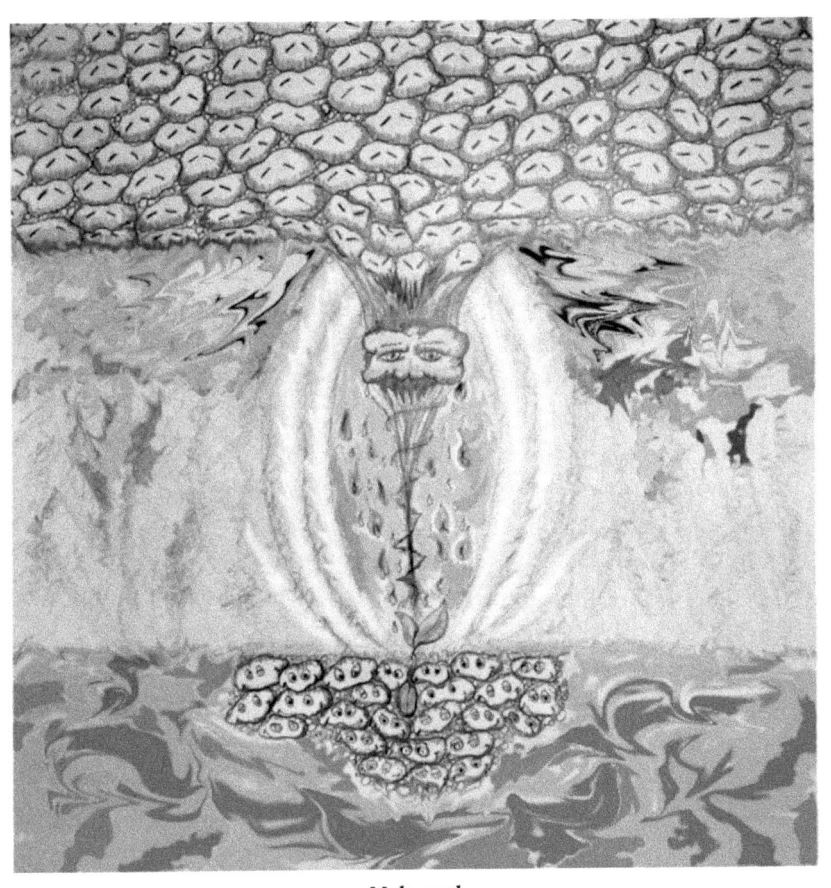

Molecruel

# Thought III

Polarized emotion has a symmetry to a thermodynamic property known as entropy. Entropy is the amount of disorder in a specific control system. A scientific law, the second law of thermodynamics, states that the entropy of a system can never decrease on its own. That is, there needs to be an application of work or action to give something order. In the following paragraph, I present a concept I have dubbed "entropic emotion theory."

Love requires one to work and learn to evolve to continue bearing it, comparable to putting work into a system to counter entropy or disorder. Hate becomes the analogous disorder in the system. Things naturally follow a path of disorder, just like one is prone to falling victim to hate if no work, or emotional evolution, is applied. If one applies effort, one can find and harness love and expunge hate. Maintaining love is, therefore, a sedulous practice.

The following poem, *WaveZ*, concerns the connection of two people. We are all waves of energy flowing, connecting, and sharing information. The flow of love, philia, in particular, helps connect us. Through philia, we can evolve towards pragma.

# WaveZ

We rode together
On a wave . . .
At crest, the sun was rising
Gravity yet to grab at us
We floated in unison
We are one
One at the peak
Our past dissipating in the trough
The vortices accelerating the time behind us
It is through
We're just beginning—the future is our perpetual energy
We're rising, and the world is falling
Our alliance gaining momentum
The shore closing in . . .
Not to crash
But to transform and add the next step
Our bond, the thin layer of surf
To shield the abrasive sand
Each grain, the ones who aren't
We can be slowed down
But not stopped
It's now up to us to keep *us* going
We have to push forth
Push, crawl, walk
So our knots are
Not for naught . . .

WaveZ

# Part Two
## The First Drop

# Thought IV

Hate is not usually innate. There's a moment in one's primordial life where hate first drips its venom. That drop has a ripple effect that poisons the spirit. It may be diluted in the waters of love if the pool of one's love is deep enough. But eventually, that drip becomes not poison, but a drug for someone. Hate begins to feel better than love, like pent-up anger being released in a fit of rage. It becomes easier than love to produce.

Hate likes to pull up a seat right behind our eyes, providing itself with a foremost visual of the prejudice it has created. One of the main forms of this prejudice is racism. It is the most visually striking and evident of the prejudices, especially for one growing up in America. It was my first glimpse of how evil a person could be and how deep hate can run, deeper than the marrow.

In the following poem, *Vociferous*, the hate portrayed is racism. This particular racism is unique to the United States. It is hate buoyed by a vile lake fed by a river of generational evil. It deals with the screams, unheard or uncared for, of the slaves during and after emancipation, which are still silenced to this day.

## Vociferous

The screams were far away
The screams were not of joy

The screams were muffled
The screams were not understood

The screams were punished
The screams were killed

The screams worked and worked
The screams worked not for themselves
        But for them over there

The screams were heard by some
The screams were set "free"

The screams traveled over the lands
The screams were felt by some

The screams never died down
The screams were on the run

The screams tried to blend with the noise
The screams settled down until new days

The screams almost bordered ecstatic
The screams didn't realize the fall in the loophole

The screams were scammed
The screams were always gonna be
        Ignored

# Thought V

If the hate is caught early and is driven away by love, one can keep the dam strong against hate's torrent. But hate will be on the other side, waiting to burst the dam open and overcome us. We all need the security of love to hold back the hate. Some people are lucky to have love all around them, acting as a metaphysical secret service.

Life is all about balance. From the act described by the title of this book to maintaining the struggle of love against hate, we have to find that balance. It is not always a binary balance; there is a ternary balance of three. We encounter a ternary balancing act with our mind, body, and spirit.

The following poem, *Mindsome*, concerns the love of self, or philautia. To love oneself, one must have a balanced mind, body, and soul. If these are equalized, and aligned, self-love can be found.

# Mindsome

The body, mind, and spirit
If the body houses the mind
The spirit frees it on an escape route
Each is necessary for one's life
Oh, the harmonious connections!
My mind can escape and travel the world
My body lies dormant
Ironic how a mind trapped in bone
Also has more freedom
More degrees of separation
My spirit intervenes
Heals my body and nurtures my mind
I look into my head to see blankness and emptiness
What a trick my body has played!

Creating an expressionless factory of expressions
In the apparent darkness of my mind, there are limitless thoughts
Bright as the eyes can muster
My spirit fuels the engine that is my mind, connects me across galaxies
My body holds my mind so it doesn't float away through the æther
It is a most perplexing paradox
The body holds the mind stagnant so it can constantly grow by the spirit
They coalesce continually through the years and maintain *me*
Without body, mind, and spirit, one is incomplete
The three *need* each other for constant survival
Self-sustaining energy
The world's most complex, yet simple, synergy
Descartes acting as a Prometheus
I think, therefore I create!

# Thought VI

For unlucky people, hate is inevitable. It surrounds and suffocates the spirit. Love—the air—just does not show at the crucial moments. This allows the hate to devour and become the dominant polar emotion. Hate is a disease. It gapes wounds. It turns the heart into a raisin in the sun. It obstinately clings to the soul like an insidious demon. It is the virus that attacks us from the inside. It is an expellant of the good we held like a postmortem-Charlton Heston rifle grip. It is pure turpitude.

## -the deadliest contagion-

Spread
By mouth
Mistreatment lubricated by
Ignorance, fear, pride, loathing
It commandeers our empty innards

Cutting
From inside
Vomited words burning
The eyes, the soul
Even then, it goes uninhibited

Sometimes
We give
Our sanity and
Sanitation away to Hell
Spew words that cut deep

Thoughts
Filthily wicked
They spread like
A disease over us
A germ pushed to others

Its
Cancer eats
Away our morals
Burns love to ashes
Killing the light within us

# Part Three
## Hate's Domination

# Thought VII

For some, hate is pushed back enough not to worry about it. This allows them to continue the fuel of love from various sources. Hate lives for this level of content. It waits to strike at an opportune time, occasionally disguised as love. One's love may be completely one-sided or too obsessive that they fall into the trap of mania, a costume hate can use.

Evil is the perpetuator of hate—the well that hate is poured into. Evil, and therefore hate, can prey on us unaware. It robs us of the little love we have in vulnerable states. It finds love at the exit and swoops in on us when weakened. It is abject in its ways.

In the following poem, *The Wise Guise*, we are exposed to hate's tactics as love is lost. It can burn mania's kindling away and cover us in ash. As love leaves, the curtain closing behind it, hate grabs our shoulder and says, "look at love leaving *us*." Meanwhile, it is latching onto our brains like a symbiont. It comes as a friend and stays as a thief in disguise, perpetually robbing us of positivity, converting it to negativity, and tossing it out at others in fear and anger.

## The Wise Guise

Masked as a one-way love affair
No reciprocation of feelings
An unhealthy obsession
A leap of faith uncaught

Lost love—hate's perfect wound
Previous obsession a delightful taste
Mania—a favored flavor of seasoning
It has prepped its feast

Hate's olfactory akin to an apex predator
Hate bites into the flesh—a cardinal carnage
It flows into the body
Wrapping its skeletal fingers around the spine

Regrets and resentments help it burrow deep
Replacing the marrow of the bone
Hate pumps into the blood
Poison masquerading as a hedonistic drug

It's the Mardi Gras beads that whip one's drunken face
Stripping the cheek to the white meat
Death comes forth in a cloak, barefaced
While hate cowers behind a vizard

We accept it because it has come to know
Our essential enfeeblement
The tendency to concede its surge
Deceit undammed by veracious love . . .

# Thought VIII

Even if love is well established, it can be driven out over time by unfortunate circumstances. Or it is decimated by puppets of hate who need others to puppeteer as part of some evil mise en abyme. As hate takes over, our ideals and character change. But hope is never lost. We always need to believe that love will eventually conquer hate. To escape being a marionette, love may fatefully find us armed with scissors to untether us from hate's bindings. Or the last bit of love we have inside us grows and grants us the strength to rip away from our strings.

The following poems represent the feeling of hopelessness due to hate and the puzzlement from receiving hate. Why would others rely on this path? Love hydrates the soul with hope. Hate can drive out hope like a diuretic forces water out of one's body. We must not let hate pound us into submission. It shall not win.

# The Evil Genie

Finally, the lamp was found.
There it was, capturing the eyes of
Three men.
Each hoping to get one wish apiece if
The fables hold.

They each placed a hand on the lamp;
They each rubbed.
The lamp clanged to the ground, burning—
Skin-meltingly hot.
Like a hiss and spray from a smoke grenade,

The genie appeared.

The genie looked down and laughed.
"Who unleashes me?"
They each raised a burnt hand.
A wish apiece, they hoped.
The genie accepted the notion.

The genie is deceiving.

The first man began to say
His wish when
The genie encapsulated him
In a tank of water.
"Ha! What is your wish?"
The genie cast an air bubble.
"I wish to get out of this tank!"

The air bubble burst,
As did the tank.
Wish granted.

Huh! Huh!

Horrified, the second man
Went to spout his wish, but the genie
Lit his shirt on fire.
The man of horrific screams
Yelled out,
"I wish for the burning to stop!"
The shirt reconfigured back to proper—
Skin anew.
Wish granted.

Huh! Huh!

Lastly, the third man,
Considering any attempt futile,
Went to walk away.
But the ground vanished.
The genie caught on to
The third man.
Falling, wailing, falling . . .
"I wish to be back on normal footing!"
Plop!
His feet landed back on previous ground.
A rattle of the lamp and the bastard was back
In his lightless limbo,
Leaving behind three traumatized men.

## The Drowning Pool

Snap!
Snap!
!!
!!


!!
!!
———

Limbs shattering
Fractures galore!
One after the other
Newborn adults were being dropped
Feet first into the

deathly shallow pool

Dropping like ripe fruit
Are they ready to rot?
Ready to plant and grow?

Broken people clutching at clumps of wet filth
Crawling, arms weak, legs broken
The tainted water just low enough
They can just breathe in spasms
Crane the neck back, pull the body forward
Where to?

As one crawls, more drop
Screams and moans in the distance
Bawling cries, balling fists
Thunderous thumps
Broken bones slammed by broken
      P eo p  l   e

Deposits into the despotism
Who brought this about?

Blood spreads through the pool
The same blood as the hangers have
The cries of precious birth
Now agony and torture

Some surrender to exhaustion
Face down and prone
Prone to their inevitable
Life never even a possibility
Drowned long ago

The Drowning Pool

# Part Four
**Middle Ground**

# Thought IX

Not only does hate tie us to its strings, it also blinds us to what love is and can be. If the strings can be severed, one's vision will still be restricted. The only escape to love and vision is now on a short tightrope. One false move and we can fall onto hate's stage and back into its possession. Conversely, all it takes is a minute step towards love to unbind us, unblind us, and leave the hate behind. Hate tries to prevent this, though, with its jailer's restraint. Hate is a controller and restricter; love sets things free.

Love can be associated with optimism, while hate is equated with pessimism. Optimism allows us to open ourselves up to the flow of love. Pessimism slams the gate shut. Although pessimism is attributed more closely to being a realist, I believe in the law of attraction. One's reality and future can drive one's outlook. An optimistic mindset can drive one to achieve the desired outcome. If one wants to be inundated by love, one simply just has to keep an optimistic outlook to gravitate towards it.

The following poem, *Blinded Fate*, invokes the torment of the absurdity of life—the pessimistic outlook. We are blinded to our own direction in life. We try to steer it the best we can, but it is sometimes like trying to solve a physical puzzle blindfolded. We have no clue how the puzzle is progressing until we take the blindfold off. When can we take it off? What is our progress on our puzzle of life? It is difficult to be optimistic about this situation, but as long as one keeps hope in mind, one has a chance to adapt and overcome any obstacle.

# Blinded Fate

All I can smell is the reeking sweat filling the room
My eyes are darkness at every angle my spine twists
Clammy hands clutch at the table, fingers slimy
I go to clasp my hands together, but I feel a sharp-edged
                Cu
                Be
I trace my fingers around and feel its fractal indentions
I try to crush it; that's all I know to do
A booming voice grounds me like a lumbered tree
"Solve this mystery!"
"No peaking!"

I hear what must be others in a frenzy
I am not alone!
Quickly, I try to identify the cube
Flipping and caressing its three dimensions—so equal
A plane twists in my contained furor

A whack of a truncheon on my back
"Swifter! You haven't aligned anything!"
I cannot speak, lips sewn shut
I grunt in despair and puzzlement
My fingers flipping planes—mind full of pain

I realize I cannot postulate where I am
We could all be in an attic or a basement
Subjects to this display of abasement
What are we all here for?
What kind of ignorance do I possess?

A twist—a neck crack
A slip—a dome check
A flip—a finger flog
A shake—a wrist whip
A slam—a turned-over chair

Lying, eyes starting to saturate the blindfold
I cannot do this task
I do not understand it
No instructions except to hasten
A kick to the stomach to regurgitate

I have to swallow not my pride
But my bile-tasting soul
Is this what life has come to?
Suffering through riddles and puzzles
With an inane bane of consciousness

# Thought X

The Greek philosopher Empedocles proposed that there are two main forces aside from the forces caused by the fundamental elements: earth, air, water, and fire. These forces were love and strife, with strife being a form of hate. Love is the attractive force; hate (strife) is the repulsive force. These forces of love and hate battle each other constantly, using us as vessels. Opening our hearts allows us to wield this attractive force. When we close off our hearts, the flow is reversed, and we repulse connections to our fellow beings. In tactile terms, love provides a warm aura for others to embrace, while hate is a cold smoke irritating the flesh.

The thing about forces is that they don't consider the human mind or, more precisely, human decision-making. The forces have a plan set out only for us to muck it up because of our free will. Free will is not alone. Our expectations of the future can also direct the forces.

In the following poem, *Breeching*, expectations are not fulfilled. This may result in a let-down, which, in turn, can lower the force of love and increase the force of hate in the form of disappointment. Disappointment can dissipate with positive proceedings or fester and allow hate to brew if left unattended.

The poem to follow *Breeching*, *LoHatVe*, is an extreme look at the cup-half-full-versus-half-empty scenario. All of Empedocles's forces are relevant. The force of love being the optimism of a half-full outlook, while the force of hate is the pessimism of a half-empty outlook. Also, the four elements come into play: the water of the half-full; the air of the half-empty; the fire of the burning strife; and the earth—the glass (sand) holding the water and air.

# Breeching

Push!
First, the feet—what makes us grounded
Push!
The legs—to travel to and fro
Push!
The tortuous torso takes time
Push! Push! Push!
The chest holds the treasure
Push!
The shoulders—heavy is the weight
Push!
Eyes bright—binary stars could not match
Push!
Life once was or a life yet to be?
Push!
The top of the head could now be seen
Push!
What a crown!
Push! Push! Push!
A scream, a cry—to be alive?
Why, yes!
A push that rolls life down its chaotic hill?
No!
The lid of the tomb pushed too mightily
A foot and a hope crushed with crumbling stone . . .

# LoHatVe (Lo-Hat-Vay)

Warmth rises given a certain gravity
The cold falls and hits bottom

Water for wash floats away from
The oil—dirt speckled

Optimism pushes the soul past
Pessimism pulls one down into a piss pore

A soft cloud to rest the mind
The hardened rock crashing against the body

A smile projected to another
A scream of agony to be alive

The scene from a tower
The long, frightening fall

Hate is an acquired taste
Love is the sugar on the "pretty please"

Hate's the haze on the horizon
Love is the sunlight on the path

Hate triggers fear and anger
Love inspires joy and respect

Hate covers the heart in putrefaction
Love polishes it into scintillation

Hate burns the beauty away—staying for the scorch
Love enhances the beauty—raising one's hope as a torch

Hate is the blood dripping from the cross
Love is the immaculate conception

To balance between the two, an eternal war
Annihilating each other like particles and anti-particles

This dichotomous struggle
Good and evil—the catalysts

What a choice
We all have

LoHatVe

# Part Five
## Singularity

## Thought XI

If family and so-called friends do not provide a vehicle to love, we may be delivered to it through the singular love of another person by falling in love. This presents a new tightrope because we can easily fall into mania, hate's relative disguised as a component of love. It is the destructive variant of love that rises high but falls hard.

In the three following poems, there will be ludus, eros, pragma, and a touch of mania. These types of love can create a singularity amongst two people. A singularity because these forms of love spiral in tight, and their forces are ineffable. They can be as extreme as infinity with an all-or-nothing approach.

# Dream Girl

I met my dream girl in a string of nightmares
Ironic, but it's just the right amount of—
Love needs to work on its timing for
People won't ever trust it

I met my dream girl in a shoddy slumber
She pulled me from the depths
The unwell well from which I fell
Was it the catch she hoped for?

I met my dream girl waking up, heart racing
The empty bed, my isolation
She was not made for me
But we were made for life together

In a dream or reality?
If we can endure each other's ephialtes,
Can we slumber fondly together?
Entangled since the quantum

May we one day end up
Side x Side

# Our Freedom Cage

The vast, open air resting on the sunken land
Both having enormous range
Spacious, yes, but how suffocating?
All this room with nothing to provide
Freedom bears such harsh irony
I look on with emptiness to reflect my sights
There's one place I long to be . . .
Far from here in

The cage of seclusion

A cage holding a pair of souls
Hers and mine
It's our terminal, our final displacement
You see, I do not desire that open space
All that's worthy would be adjacent to my heart
To be in arm's reach
It's the perfect zone
Our world within a world
Smaller in size, but grander in might
Its gravitation is unparalleled
Securing the door without a lock
I could not, nor would I, dare to leave it
I stay
We stay
Jovial and warm as the cold air flows past
The land beneath our feet solid on a fluid earth
Our cage with bars holding in the passion radiating
      From our collective countenances

Not a prison of our own doing, a shelter for our love
Pure amusement floods the cage, pulled in by it
Together is our purpose
Our bodies stagnant, our attraction inflating
Nothing should save us from this place
Here, justly content forever
Nothing can compare to
        Our Freedom Cage

Our Freedom Cage

# Forged

Dead penetrating the sights
Shifter of life
Unknown direction on a single path
At first a cry, and now a laugh
Given up within the initial memories
Scraping along, suffocated by the discrepancies
Thoughts vivid—placing stepping stones in front
Hinder the pain, never give up
Reaper avast, narrow the plane
Hoping for that last insane
Effulgence overwhelms the crepuscular aura
Given sight of Her
A gracious gift waiting for this
She who overcame
A prize of wealth to deplete the shame
Loneliness can only make it so far
We all carry its salted scar
When the drifter is obtained by Her
She'll find it is a seasoned sir
A man of what She has seen
A man who has reoccurred in many dreams
What will *they* do once They unite?
Companionship to progress each enlightened?
Wherever They go, changes will be the friction that enables
Equilibrium
All Their essence melts away the malice
From the dark beginnings of separate origins
To the future of great and sacred fortunes
The Two will ignite all that's relevant
Forever, They'll create an immortal element

Part Six
# The Getting Up

# Thought XII

The most arduous love to achieve is agape. Since love itself can be difficult for people in hateful and negative circumstances, obtaining just one of the nine loves is not easy. This love adds selflessness, which is hard to achieve on its own. One has to deflate one's ego to begin the process of reaching agape. To practice agape, one needs to open up entirely to the world and allow a highway of love and acceptance to travel uninhibited.

    The following poem, *The Eternal Epiphany*, demonstrates that love is difficult to grasp if the right components aren't in place. We may need that "aha!" moment to allow benevolent external forces to push us towards love dominance and a magnanimous nature.

Winds of change blow through your soul
Almost knocking
        You off
                balance
Your head clears; your mind numbs
The somber melancholy that once consumed you
        Is justly carried away
                          by the zephyr
The numbness fades like the eroded stoneToo close
To the combative elements
In an instant, your knees give, and you find your body
                                    Fall-
                                      ing
But the breeze alters noitcerid/direction
Almost lifts you back to its initial positionWinds of change . . .
The same wind that nearly knocked you towards the end
Trans f o r m s into the wind that terminated the plunge
It's in that moment . . .

Wind is love
A fling over
        feet
At first
But a catch to finalize

## The Eternal Epiphany

# Thought XIII

If love is accepted and maintained, hate can be driven out—but not for good. We must always stay vigilant to keep it at bay. We will always tread that thin line, that tightrope. But if we choose to harness ourselves with positivity instead of negativity, a slip and fall won't be destructive. We must always be willing to take that step across to love and away from hate.

Hate does not have to be the dominant polar emotion. We can abolish it with the right storm of positivity and support. As shown in the following poem, *The Bigot Tree*, hate/strife may stand tall, but it can be overcome with love. Hate can be drowned out by the flood of love's precipitation.

# The Bigot Tree

The land flooded
Flooded with great knowledge
But the ornery tree stood
It could not take the change
The difference alerted a histamine battalion
It dropped poisonous fruits
Used the water to continue hating
To thrive and become a bigger tree

The relentless water kept its torrent
It heightened and heightened
To the Bigot Tree's dismay
The flood almost covered the tree
This rainy, sepulchral day was a precursor to
The Big Change

The clouds, how they came together
With thunder, they spoke
With lightning, they struck close
No preparation for persistent precipitation
The waves crashed into its weakened trunk
These clouds raised the tide themselves

It was now submerged, save a leaf
It could not drink its way out of this
Its roots no use
The flood was winning
The biggest growth this tree ever need
To drown this hideousness in the abyss

Drowned by the maturation of its whereabouts
The biggest stick-in-the-mud
Its relationship with the sun severed
The light taken
Taken back with
Waves unbroken . . .

The Bigot Tree

# Thought XIV

Once love is found and kept, it warms the heart. It melts the icy hate away like the first sun after a winter storm. Hate has tried to besmirch what we were born with in an attempt to detract from our true potential. Love can be lost, but it can also be found. Whether it be through reopening the relationship with a higher power or finding that person who tears the hinges off the door to our heart, love will flow as fiercely as the flood of melting snow on that long-awaited vernal day.

In the following poem, *Above*, the hate/strife of others and the hate imbedded in one's heart are driven out by the force of love. Hate is cast away from us, but we learned about the value of love from our trek with hate. Hate provides an energy that can be morphed into love with the correct emotional tools, developing mindset, and external assistance.

# Above

The fire from above
Not to destroy, but to employ—that is love
Overall beauty storming
Corroding the faces with that other madness
It tends to kill the sadness

The sight of the sky eliminates boundary
A road for the souls to travel when called
This land of wonder—a seductive ignorance
What force do we have?

Simultaneous pulses obligate the belief
Series of warm echos against the skin
She is back again!

Her fate upon me shall force the will
No wrong images described by either tongue
No war between us, nothing won nor lost

Simple and contagious, her overpowering light
It casts my shadow but burns away the darkness

Her love is a soaking downpour from the heavens
It is now our shield

Our destiny, has it been forged?
Doesn't the frigid and rigid slate get warm after a perfect engraving?

Our passion would melt that rock into transparency
The medium that hate tried to hide

So long as we ride the Moon through the tide
We will always see each other's bright side

# Part Seven
## As the Sun Sets

# Thought XV

Our understanding of the tactics of love and hate grows with experience and developed heuristics. Some people die hateful; some die with love spilling out of their hearts. There is a trite saying, "you can't teach an old dog new tricks." But with the right effort, surroundings, and people, this saying can be nullified.

The duality of reality is proposed in *LoHatVe* with the different perspectives of half full and half empty. Some of the main subjects of Part Seven are reality's duality and incorporating new love past the early learning portion of life or in life's later stages.

The sun creates a moment of duality. A setting sun can be viewed as leaving or disappearing. But over a body of water, its other half is reflected. At that brief moment of half gone, half appearing, the reflection perfectly replicates the other half, resulting in an image of a complete sun.

The following poems describe the nature of reality, in particular its duality. Life's duality can be driven by the battle of the opposing forces of love versus hate, true versus false, or good versus evil. It is up to us as part of our reality to help the positive side overcome the negative.

# Dam of Reality

Looking at the etching
It cuts into the background
All of it severing the dam of reality

No more of this seclusion
The rusted chain has been fractured
Some passerby fixed the skipping record

The repetition has been terminated
Extreme of frontiers has been pushed towards its new boarders
A flood of unknown crashes onto the ignorant lives

Washes the filth created by the idiotic institution we've all been enlisted to
Who would have considered our dimensions configured for a cage?
We've spread out spatially, but to no avail

None of it mattered or would have
Our prolific ascension provides necessity
New found necessity and vision

See, before we were senseless, blind most of all
Here we were blind, trying to hurt and destroy one another
But a switch has been made—grandeur

A mind revelation for everyone soon to be cast in this divergent reality
It's not a new dimension; they don't exist any longer
We are no longer blind, deaf, or numb

Reflections are now the fresh reality
Life bursting from the light
How will we fare with this resurrection?

Will we become a race of higher magnitude?
Time's elegant river will proceed to speak
Now that the dam of reality has been reaped . . .

# Fantastic Fabric

It runs through us like rivers
We are mills of the undamned
We are carved and sewn into it
The falsehoods bounce around the quilt
Never to be incorporated
But to go from one patch to the next
Tumbling, trying to cover truths
Damming the flow, damping its momentum
This textile will never stop, no matter the impediments
The truth *is* the fabric
This eternal blanket that covers us through the night
The canvas that blocks the rays too bright
The strands may fray and split
Fluttering in the gusts of
The false breaths
They may never stain it with their stale saliva
Fantastic fabric vines through vibrations
Like the cocoon of a moth
It is our vital cloth

# Thought XVI

Becoming selfless has contradictory aspects. We have to selfishly pursue it at times and grow in solitude. For example, in the final step of the twelve-step recovery from addiction, one ultimately becomes selfless and exudes agape to help others. But that same person must "selfishly" take the time to be alone and become mentally reborn.

Xenia is a gateway to agape. As one becomes more hospitable, one practices selflessness. Recovery from addiction is rooted in xenia because helping strangers who are also in recovery is part of the recovery process. Once one has practiced enough xenia and understands it, one can ascend to agape. Both xenia and agape are related to altruism. As an addict in recovery and fellow human being, one must invest in altruistic thinking. We all need help, and we all need love.

In the following poem, *Nine Out of Twelve*, perfectionism, which is greatly tied to one's ego, is reined in. Perfectionism, at its extreme, is a form of self-loathing or self-hatred. The self-abuse of perfectionism eases once one allows self-love. This results in a more balanced and healthier ego. When the mind and the heart are balanced and healthy, selflessness can be cultivated. We must learn to forgive and love ourselves in order to love others. If we have resentments toward ourselves, we cannot let go of the faults and mistakes of others and love purely.

# Nine Out of Twelve

Perfection would be twelve out of 12
Seven7y-5ive percent is still passing, right?
But it's never enough

How can i exist if i cannot fulfill?
An immense hOle larger than myself
Cannot be filled with a drink or a pill

                        i jump over hurdles that are behind me
                            If i just quit looking in the mirror
                                   i can move forward

              Was my potential an Everest peak?
        For me to transfer kinetically into an abhorrent crash
            I pick up the pieces—my pulchritudinous m
                                         c
                                      s
                                  a
                             o
                                  i

# Afterword

By breaking down love, as the ancient Greeks did, we can further understand what it is. Through the perspective of the nine loves; philia, pragma, eros, ludus, storge, philautia, agape, mania, and xenia, the deep layers of love are peeled away. The remaining core is left to be defined by each individual. My core of love is the source of positive emotions and desires. The more we dissect love and gain understanding, the more we can understand its counterpart, hate. Hate is layered the same way as love, with its core definition being subjective. I define hate as a negative source of emotions, with its main components being internal hate and external hate.

Love is the sustenance for all our positive emotions. Through love, we feel joy, hope, satisfaction, and tranquility. Hate is the source of our negative emotions. It allows for fear, sadness, and anger to dominate our feelings. Although we cannot completely rid ourselves of negative emotions, we can cultivate love to strengthen our positive emotions and limit the effects of negative emotions. If love is cultivated deeply and robustly, it empowers us, while hate is a parasite that attaches to and ruins the soul.

The progression of society as a whole has not been up to par in the areas of love and hate. Our technological progression has exceeded our evolution of emotions. It may be a universal tradeoff that as technology ascends higher, we devolve as a society. It has become an easier idea for one to travel to the Moon than to travel to another's heart. It is within our power to balance this trend by spreading love and acceptance aboundingly.

This declining trend coincides with the weakening of xenia love. Xenia is becoming an antiquated love, with hospitality becoming scarcer. We are losing respect for others and ourselves. If we begin to respect the human plight, the hardship of being alive, we can regain some stability in love. Hate feeds on our neurotic decay and pushes people away. We need to offer our hand and become more altruistic. This would be the first step towards an emotional revolution.

Positive human connections are the foundations for love. Through developing connections, we are pushed through a current of positive emotions. Negative emotions can be felt out of love, such as sadness at the death of a loved one. Hate is ready to pounce on the vulnerable. It constricts and topples the love once built for that person when the primary emotion concerning their death becomes an unhealthy sadness. We must look out for each other whenever possible.

Love is the hero of the story of life. Hate is the villain that love must defeat. The struggle may be eternal, but we can always have faith that love will conquer hate one day. It will require the help of every individual to take a stand against hatefulness. A collective consciousness that accepts love over hate will be necessary. It will be extremely onerous to execute. I have hope it can be done. Hope is the dew on the seed of love . . .

• • •

The following appendix is a collection of poems that delve into mania. Some were composed by myself during a time of one-way loves. The rest are from a dear friend, Philip Crichton. He became so enamored with another person that he forgot to love himself. His love for the other person became more important than his next breath. This is the type of love that can be as destructive and negative as hate itself. We must be able to reel ourselves back once we feel the onset of mania love. Mania has the power to drive one to solely focus on the other person, or on oneself under extreme narcissism. It becomes destructive to the person applying the mania and to the person receiving it. Love is the warmth of the fire, but mania is the burn when getting too close to the flame.

# Appendix
## Mania Collection

# Envy Us

On the day we were first introduced, the envy began to brew
Deep inside the center of space, it grew and grew
'Til our hearts began to thrive wildly, it kept its place far away
Once we became forever united, it came out of the depths and traveled this way

Like a desperate politician, it devoured those that paused in its presence
Everything around us became under its grim influence
First steps for our everlasting enemy
Feeding off all we have—to save itself from the deadly empty

The clouds resting in the skies
Could not rain hard enough to display its true cries
The moon of the Earth could not drown us with its tides
The wind of the seas could not blow a gust of lies

Blindly envying what we have between our hearts
It did not know the strength of all our parts
It did not know what it was envying could not be faltered
Neither damaged nor weakened nor altered

It tried to turn an army against our rarity
It tried to use negativity as the universal charity
It tried tactics known only to those who've seen struggles vanish
It failed to defeat our union with much anguish

Now, here we stand . . . Alone
As the envious being has withered dry as a bone
Our land normal to its previous fate
One thing remains
       There cannot, nor will there ever, be a two together so great

# Remedial

You remember the first time I made you laugh?
Or the first time I made you smile?
You remember the first time you got impatient when I told you I'd call you
        After while?
Remember the time you couldn't get me out of your head?
Or the time we talked so much we never went to bed?
You remember the first time I took your breath away?
Or the time you had to count down the days?
Remember the look in my eyes the first time we met?
Or how everything we did, or will ever do, you'll never
        Regret?
You remember when you acted like a dork and lightened the times?
Or when you fell in love because you saw the signs?
Remember how happy you were to be labeled "us?"
Or when we first held hands on the shuttle bus?
Remember how we went crazy and made mistakes?
Or when we corrected them and made it all great?
You remember the first time you told me you loved me?
Or when we felt they couldn't replicate us in
        A movie?
Remember that it's us forever
And know that we'll always be together

# Is it?
by Philip Crichton

The sound of your heart captivates my ears
The elegance of your body enslaves my eyes
The intense nature of your mind mystifies my thoughts
The movement of your body makes water appear as ice
Your smile electrifies my soul
I dream about the touch of your body
I believe it will make the sun appear as a glacier and silk feel gritty
All this dances in my mind, and I think to myself:
"Is it possible that our hearts can beat to the same note?"
"Is it possible we can stop time?"
"Is it possible to be infatuated with someone as such?"
"Is it possible to get lost and find each other in the same darkness?"
"Is it possible to go blind but only see each other?"
"Is it possible to save each other from falling?"
"Is it possible to never worry again because we are together?"
Impossible died the moment we locked eyes . . .

# Our Vehicle
by Philip Crichton

We're flowing down the path as if it were a river
The road winds and meanders
No dead end, no crossroads—just a single path
We have no idea where the path leads
Neither do we know how we got on
Fate or hope, maybe

We occupy the same vehicle
We feel the same bumps
The same turns
The same turbulence
We both feel the wind pressing against our faces
And the sun shining down through parted clouds

The rain, however, cannot enter our open vehicle
No one is steering; it seems to be automated
The road is empty, save us
We keep moving forward
Peaceful and safe
Onward with each other

# Physics Broken
by Philip Crichton

Light speeds up just to reflect off your beauty
The air slows its motion to caress your soul
The earth becomes softer to your footsteps
Not allowing a rough path
The skies fall to touch you
The angels envy your grace
Sugar loathes your taste
My heart weeps to want you
There's not a single word that can contain you
Not love nor your name
You are the point of no return and
The force that blocks the past
Dreams cannot tell me how wonderful you are
Nor the elements can equate your presence
The outsiders can contest
But your beauty cannot be less

# Force Not Farce

by Philip Crichton

It's uncanny, this feeling
I cannot be stopped
I'm like a juggernaut bullet
Or like an unobstructed comet

I feel relevant to everything
Freedom has taken over
Love is consuming
Fear is lost and senseless
Weak as a mosquito to an explosion

Nothing can touch me
But there is one exception

She's by my side
She's the one who gave me this strength
She's propelling me onward

I'm clutching her hand
Fingers forcefully fused together
I'll never let go

We'll never let go

It's her and me forever—unstoppable
Unfathomed fearlessness we possess
Space expands to our will
Time becomes irrelevant

# Her Fact
by Philip Crichton

There's no light, and all she hears is cacophony
Harsh but empty sounds of erroneous souls
They judge without perception
They are blind to her impression
She walks through the darkness not knowing if she's as
Blind as them
But a correction runs through her veins like a substitute for
        Adrenaline
There's a faint light drawing ever closer
At her feet, a puddle of tears left by the ignorants
She sees her reflection with the aid of that faint light
        Growing ever brighter
Excitement fills any present emptiness
Darkness now lies behind her
The light blinding with the strength of its apex
Contradiction holding, the light dims at the end of her tunnel
Now dimmed to an equilibrium
The light brings a gift to her eyes
The puddle
The puddle with an image
The image—a sight exciting the eyes to tears
The tears wash away the disbelief
The disbelief cowering in her mind is unclasped and dropped
It strikes the puddle, but it does not disturb the image
Her beauty and aura never wavering
Though ignorant minds will try and fade the image
They can never defeat her fact

# Sinceless
by Philip Crichton

I think something is ghastly wrong
I can't feel anything
I can't see anything
Nor can I hear
My heart is overwhelmed with panic
A new type of scared

Then there's a touch
I feel the fingertips of an angel
I can now see her face
I can now hear her voice
And the satisfying rhythm of her heartbeat

Abruptly, this all ends
I revert to my initial stage
No senses, I can barely think
Darkness sets in, overcoming my soul

If my blood left my body
I wouldn't know
And I wouldn't care

Something hits my conscious like a
Meteor bent on extinction

I alone cannot bring back my senses

Only she—my lone hope
        This angel, this goddess
                May she ever return . . .

# Twin Hearts
by Philip Crichton

I wonder onward through the thicket
The air is scarcely breathable, and the light has met
    Its match
All I need is to find my way, lose the uneasiness of
    My mind
I blissfully recognize a previous vision
Have I been retracing my pedium?
Calmness leaves my person like dew off a blade of grass
    At the peak of the helio
Will I find my way, my path to righteousness?

I do not lose all my aplomb or ambition, but my mind is ailing
Each step appears as its predecessor
Am I reaching any gain?
A sharp light pierces the forest, a source of warmth to
    Battle Lord Kelvin
Initial blindness crazes my cranium
Another edge to my blade, perhaps
A figure emerges from the light
She is elegant and peaceful

Her presence is all that is necessary for strengthened hope
Her majestic atmosphere—the peak of beauty
She provides her hand, and we
    Float about in the chaos that is
She delivers me sanity
I am in a vast field now
My sight burns back into my eyes

I look around, and she has vanished!
A slight panic overcomes me
Where is my savior?

I feel the beating of twin drums in my chest
Courage is the man with two hearts
Never again will I travel alone

# Her Name (Our Nature)
by Philip Crichton

The waves erode the shore
> but it is imperceptible

Lives are changed everyday
> but sometimes unfelt

Subtleties rule the world
> rudiments swirling in a

Complex arena

Like how *you* can make my heart excited for the next beat
Like how *our* gravity out-duels the Earth to pull *us* together

The intensity in *your* eyes that fills me with a profound trust in *you*
I forget that everything around *us* matters

Now, looking at the tremors that direct my soul
I am brought to a plain of peace and warmth
> Your solar prominence transferring me there

It is here in this land that I find myself
It is here that I become illiterate

Because I spell every word that bears any magnitude:
O-L-I-V-I-A

# When Wings Crawl
by Philip Crichton

The sky is dim, overcast
Stale light penetrates here and there
Severing the moist, cool air
Nature well aware of the present
Gloom so soon
Drops of Poseidon's particles fill the troposphere

Animals seek shelter
Some have not the proper dwellings
In particular, the wingéd one
She is too far from boughs when the earth becomes water
No place to go, let it not be the end!
Nothing left for her now

Hope is now an alien
Everything is turned to darkness, save for its foe-ton
The light that couldn't give up
It grows against the lost feeling
It is winning
It's driving the wingéd one, not the air

Not the air that hosted this deadly water
Not the air that betrayed the wingéd one

But minuscule light—it lifts her
Hope now descending back to earth
The wings lifted towards harmony
Towards the heavens and away from the water

Will the wings and hope intersect?
Hope will not crash, will it?

The light that grows begins to dim
Her flight reducing
The droplets like bullets wounding
Her mind falling faster than the altitude
Nihilism pulling her down
Above a vast body of water

The insignificance of her struggle—of her existence
Is it over?

The light, not the gleam from armor but the
Knight itself, pushes her through the surface
With a fountain-like splash, she emerges
Catching hope as it lands on her wings
Light rising
Her thoughts in complete revolution

Could it be that the wingéd one can survive submersion?
Light and hope becoming timely shields?

She is not of the ordinary
The creature with the most amazing transformation
This particular butterfly with a metamorphosis of the mind
Hope will not crash
Darkness cannot drown her
And she will never give up

# Upon Opening
by Philip Crichton

It's happening again
That trapped feeling
I look up at the sky and see free-moving clouds of string
Birds aflight, light dominating everything
Except down here, it's dark
It's frigid and dreary
I see the faint outline of a door
Or maybe just an awkward rectangle of misplaced hope
I walk towards it, scraping away the curiosity on every step
The light burning through the cracks of the door provide
A flare for the gilded doorknob
I reach for it, hoping it's the answer to me being trapped
It's an icy touch, a derma-frost
But I clench and try to twist it
I try and try, but to no avail
The door is locked
My grip gone the way of the dinosaurs
I feel ultimately trapped
Frozen on the outside with the cold and gloom
A mere instant before I lose all hope, the door swings wide
The light burns my eyes
Am I not worthy?
There's a silhouette of someone, someone hoarding beauty
My eyes and mind adjust
All I can handle is the potential
      Oh! The grace!
It's *her*, the woman I have pictured my whole life
I've imaged her in this vast prison—my prison

She's here to finally bring me inside
Inside the door to light, to warmth, to love—*me*—a stranger
She has saved me, relieved me from my hopelessness and Dis-
    Honor
Without a word or a proper exchange, she becomes my anything
    And everything
I worship her, for she has been the spark of life, the kindle in my soul
    I always needed
My life finally begins—decades after birth . . .

Printed in the USA
CPSIA information can be obtained
at www.ICGtesting.com
LVHW051552250823
756268LV00006B/141